THE BIG JUMP FROM WHITE LIES

WRITTEN BY
SIMION WRIGHT & SASHANA ANDERSON

ILLUSTRATED BY
MONIKA MARZEC

We would like to dedicate this book to
children all around the world.
Always tell the truth because it is what
will set you free.
Your conscience will be clear.

"Hey Paul, do you know what happened to me ten minutes ago, before you got here?" asked John.
Paul replies, "No John, what happened?"

John then said, "I was
running towards the door
to my bedroom, bumped
my toe and flipped down
the stairs."
Paul pauses for a little
while and thinks to himself,
is this true what John said?

After careful thought Paul says, "there is no evidence to work with, but I will take a closer look to see if there is any evidence of bruises or scratches on your lower body. I cannot tell if your story is truthful. Your facial expression is showing something different from what I am seeing right now."

Paul says to John, "John, you know you are my best friend, and you must not make up stories or lies, just to look good for the moment?

"I guess you are right," said John, with a bright smile. He then continues to say, "Yes, I know that my mom trusts you to be my friend, and a good example in my life as well."

In every good relationship there are lies and truths, but it's up to us to see the difference."

John said to Paul in a soft and humbled voice, "Lies will only lead to mistrust and resentment between two good friends when one of them starts to lie."

"I believe you Paul," said John. "You remind me of a story that my father said his father told him when he was a little boy. It was about a shoemaker who received a letter to make a shoe for an old lady. She was travelling from Jamaica to London.

She wrote a letter saying:

Hi Mr. Shoemaker,

I am unable to come to your shoe shop at this time; I am home with my grandkids doing housework. I need you to make me shoes and the letter contains the size of my feet. Please work with the drawing and don't make the shoes size bigger or smaller, but make the shoes beautiful.

"So, the shoemaker did as the old lady asked."

"When she received the shoes, she was so happy; but when she wore the shoes, she was so sad.

As soon as she took the shoes
off her feet and held them in
her hands, she was very happy
again."

Paul asks John, "What is the meaning of this story John? I still don't get it."

John replies, "Sometimes, the truth is right in front of you, just for you to believe and receive it. Instead, we ignore the truth, which brings us light and joy; that can take away our sorrows and heal our pain.

Paul says, "I'm still hoping to understand the mystery of the story you told me, but I still don't get it John. Paul you are the one at fault here."

John replies, "Yes Paul, I did mix the truth with lies and I was wrong. I'm asking you to forgive me for my lies and deceitfulness. I am very sorry and hope that you will give me a chance to regain your trust again as my friend."

"John my friend," said Paul. "I forgive you; I love you and we are not perfect. Come on, let's go play tag."
John asks Paul, "Can I tell you my side of the story, what really happened?"

Paul replies, "Yes John, you can tell me."
John explains "I was in the backyard, where I was jumping up and down on the stairs around the deck. Then, I tripped on a brick in the grass, fell over and scratched my leg."
"I believe you John," said Paul. "Ok, fair enough. Now let's go play. We can continue this discussion about the old lady and her shoes next time," Paul said to John, as they both walked away smiling.
John replies, "Yes!"

John finishes off by saying, "I hope that boys and girls around the world will learn from our story; to both forgive others and to ask for forgiveness.

Always tell the
truth and be brave
about it regardless
of the
consequences you
face in life."

www.ingramcontent.com/pod-product-compliance
Lightning Source LLC
Chambersburg PA
CBHW042142030726
47599CB00002B/590